The Way I Remember It

Essential Poets Series 56

Antonino Mazza

The Way I Remember It

Guernica

Montreal, 1992

Antonio D'Alfonso, editor.
Guernica Editions Inc.
P.O. Box 633, Station N.D.G.
Montreal (Quebec), Canada
H4A 3R1

The publisher gratefully acknowledges the financial
assistance from The Canada Council and Le ministère
des Affaires culturelles du Québec.

Legal Deposit — First Quarter
National Library of Canada and Bibliothèque nationale du Québec.

Canadian Cataloguing in Publication Data

Mazza, Antonino
The way I remember it

(Essential poets; 56)
Poems.
ISBN 0-920717-74-8

I. Title. II. Series.
PS8576.A99W39   1992   C811'.54   C92-090049-6
PR9199.3.M39W39   1992

Contents

*To Angela Busceti and Domenico Mazza
whose work this is as much as our own.*

Introduction

*God pushed a boat into the mouth of the sun
and our planet began to swim.*

In and out of the light, the milky waves....

The Way I Remember It is a collaboration between two brothers, two artists, who have over a number of years produced works, one in poetry, the other in music. The album is the result of their personal dialogue about alienation, a condition shared by anyone who has been swept onto foreign shores.

As large migrations continue to pour into our cities, we have seen a gradual fusion of diverse cultures fold into one gigantic, homogenizing civilization intent on swallowing up all differences. Too soon we forget that old cultures embody a living aesthetic: spiritual values that make life worth living. It seems more and more that the only way of safeguarding these traditions is to preserve them in libraries and museums like relics of the past. We feel less and less capable of seeing ourselves reflected in them as our own. Such is the condition of alienation that results from the separation of 'anthropological memory' and 'self'.

These works inform us that it need not be so. Within every one of us, no matter what our origins, is hidden a timeless, submerged map that can provide a renewed perspective, and lead us back to a sense of personal integrity.

We cannot return to the past. But, in defying the direction of the monolithic reductionism of the cultural status quo that in the modern era is bent on stunting our cultural regeneration, bent on nullifying diversities, we can stimulate the re-invention, the becoming, of other worlds.

This album began when I discovered my brother's interest in ethno-cultural music. One night in 1985 at his house in Montreal, he talked with enthusiasm about the timbre and rhythm of certain Asian and African percussion instruments. This invigorated me to read him some poems I had written about Calabria, a region in the southernmost part of Italy whose culture we have in common. He must have been moved by those images of our past regained. To my surprise, a couple of weeks later, I received a tape in which a poem had been magically underscored with a musical composition of electronically produced sounds, evoking the indigenous music of our ancestral region.

The course of our collaboration had thus been set. Our direction was to turn the loss of self into an instrument for appropriating the culture of the day, by adding to its repertoire our own story with its own particular ethnic codes, a story that reveals something of our diverse world.

Jorge Luis Borges remarks somewhere that it is 'only new countries that have a past, that is to say, an anthropological memory of their past, a living history'. In assembling materials for the album we experienced at first hand the truth of this seemingly paradoxical statement, as I began to collect poems remembered by Calabrians in Canada.

To our astonishment this took us to the very heart of Western literary tradition. As chance would have it, my own father, whose memory of oral poetry in the Calabrian dialect is staggering, provided me with a poem in the *altercatio* or *débat* genre. This literary type had been popular in Carolingian times and probably goes back to the pastoral eclogues of Theocritus and Virgil. This nugget, 'Si sí veru poeta di Marsigghia' (If You're a True Poet of Marseilles), which we reproduced in the album to represent a silenced past, is imbued with the themes that inform the rest of the poetry in the album: absence, deterritorialization, loss, the human condition of being the original wanderer, the feast.

The choice to include this poem in the album inspired my brother, Aldo, to acquaint himself with the intricate techniques of playing the southern Calabrian tambourine. While Aldo was preparing for this, he discovered to our surprise and delight, in my father's home in Ottawa, that my father could play Calabrian tambourine. Needless to say, that evening is an unforgettable one for us. Neither of us had ever seen our father play this instrument before. It seemed incredible to us that we had spent our lives not knowing the whys and wherefores of our own artistic and cultural inheritance.

We invite you to share in this improbable feast where past and present meet, in the conviction, to say it with Jean Cocteau, that 'the more a poet sings inside his genealogical tree, the more he sings in tune'.

Antonino Mazza
Toronto, March 1988

'Given the condition which is common to all artists today, the postmodern condition, which we might describe as essentialized in life in the metropolis, I see in Antonino Mazza a certain joyous strategy, in his very conscious understanding of his use of ethnicity as a way of interpreting, and even as a way of stepping out of the postmodern condition.'

William Boelhower
CBC Anthology

The Way I Remember It

Our House Is in a Cosmic Ear

In a cosmic ear of sharp peaks and stepped hills
  where broom and cyclamen bloom
  side by side with the lemon trees
is the house where I was born.
This house... let's look at it from a childish
                              point of view.
A village of bells crowded in the velvet street,
  no sidewalk. Sunday morning, no Monday.
How is it? I was running home, there were cherries
in my pockets, my mother had a nightingale
              between her lips?

And the afternoon? Siesta!
                    The sun
was a magnet at the summit of a transparent planet.
But the cloud? The Blazing breath of the Sahara
whirled a single cloud, over the sea,
                    over Sicily,
until, nearing the harsh Aspromonte, fragile
              with humidity, it was... ready to burst.
And Blasted!
        reaching, violently, for the stubborn stubbles,
              for earth.

After the first splatter on the baked roof,
　　the lean torrents, clay snakes,
　　wound their course, out from the birch forests,
　　　　　down the steep volcanic slopes,
　　　　　　　　slowly,
as if to admire the grace of the stern landscape: the yellow
and pink weeds glowing on the violet crags,
　　　　　and on the steppes
the white blanket of orange flowers.
Before the rain would stop, I'd retire
　　　　　　in my mother's ear, sound asleep.

For four years I dreamt of my father coming back.
　　It was a childish dream.
He was aboard a little purple ship, returning
to our beautiful Calabria.
　　　　　Phoenician's and Etruscan's land, bathed
　　　by the sea of Ulysses.
For four years I waited for him on the stony beach.
From there I could see the almonds mingling
　　　　　　with the olive trees,
　　　　　　　　　in the hills,
　　　　　and the house where he was born.
　　He had gone to bring gifts to the world.
He would return, soon.

I'd wake up to the melody of nightingales.
And the dream? It is evening, but never dark. The bells
   die in the deep blue street. The sky is a paradise
        of fireflies. The scent of lilacs, of lemons,
      flood the warmth, the breeze. The sea is a mirror
   of purple stars. We're having supper on the terrace
tonight, in the crystal air the moon is abundant light.
I keep remembering this cosmic gift

                              in my sleep.
If the dream doesn't stop, if the word,
                  if the house
   is in the word and we, by chance, should meet,
my house is your house, take it.

Muscoli

Who is that man
wrapping the moaning muscoli (arms
and back)
'ointing the chipped hands with olive oil
and still waging war
morning after morning
building and tearing buildings
after roads
iced fingers torn and bleeding between
nailed boards (like castigation splinters)
nails nailed with nails

Muscoli and minds must open the door
that's what he came here for

Never saw I a man
burn so like a torch
never heard a man
self-will to scorch
for his child

He took to his chains as he
wished I should mine in my brains
and roared at the earth like
the devil on abel
he had spirited demons at the eyes
per dio he'll make a man out of you
before he dies

Muscoli and minds must open the door
that's what he came here for

Viaggio

God pushed a boat into the mouth of the sun
and our planet began to swim.

In and out of the light, the milky waves:

the sea grew tongues the evening gathered dusk,
the light that lapped our wooden walls,
the waves that chased us, that chased the yellow
slopes, the way the sea made love to the pebbly
beach, the earth, a butterfly
                            afloat.

The night our violet earth was lost beyond a disk
of stars, our half moon was copper cup, and the heart,
inside a chest of bones, a broken child;
my ship rippling in a dish of honey: and I never
thought there'd be so much honey!

In and out of the waves, the polar chills;

it is a dream of copper sunsets, of cherished hopes,
the memory of our journey, between the daily loaves
of dread, between the whines;
                    still, it is ourselves we meet
when we meet love, when we meet our dreams: and life
becomes a dish we relish so much we don't want
to finish, if in her eyes the earth bursts back
into the waves, and our hearts break into the sunlight.

And we grow lips for a child, friend, lost
between two planets when we enter a tangle of tongues
as into a beehive to sting the sweetness and be stung.

And the chills, in and out of the waves,

the way a ship is thrust inside our rippling flesh,
the way a copper planet begins to drift towards us,
towards our lost hopes,
the way even God can't hide behind a forest
of leaves, that cheer, in and out of the light,
that feast for us, wondering souls.
                    And the chills!

But who would want to suppress a fleeting shudder
if it were a matter of arriving,
arriving home,
home   so soon   after so long?

In the Threshold

Light-greyish smoke rises and
restrains me like the evening tide;
pushed back, like a crowbar
through a broken door,
I shriek and fall to the ground.

The earth is overcast;
I enter the drainpipe like the sound of rain;
a pair of crocodile construction boots
await my descent into the sewer:
I'm black-polluted-sweptround.

In the frontlines
it's a razorblade confrontation; I'm bleeding
at the seams,
I scream: 'STOP CROWDING!'—
but I'm not relieved.

There is a corridor.
Taking the door to the left
I exit into the backyard,
the castiron staircase in the centre,
I know, leads down through the firechimney.

I stop. Roll myself enough cigarettes
for a chainsmoker,
I don't make a fuss,
I'm naked to the waist,
I'm stiff, but my hat keeps me warm.

By the bench there is a window
covered by a heavy drab.
Between silences I can hear a brook's stonejump.
— 'if it doesn't rain
I'll try to stand up, tomorrow.'

Ossobuco

The earth arrives in a village with chestnut eyes
and I can't help myself if fire pours out of my mouth.

There was a purple road once.
It now returns; wine in my head,
the way the sky spins for the evening sun.

And the volcano again breaks the horizon. But my
grandfather... the clay pipe in the orange groves
belching mouthfuls of laughter?

When I arrived, what I'd remembered most died.
But the scent of it flows, invisible through ancient
windows. Inside me, it lingers for love
with longing fingers, the way a muscle smiles, for life.

And I can't help it. The poem, filled with heart enough
to cup all bodies of water, to flood all memories
pours out of me, like a bone with a hole in it,

and I can't help it. Like a dirt road bolting uphill
my life arrives with me, in an orange forest,
and unfurls in a blaze of colours.

Paranoia

Persecuted by (the clashing of hammer
claspps) the gripping of iron for the
door to graspp

and the walls snapp together
shrinking the ceiling (the cornering
caverns a yard of cubed-air)
pressing space into the dice
constricting

and the-cat-flashed-by (the
circle of the square) almost
three-full-times and SPLATT

Giovannina

In memory of my sister

The planet moves in the wind along the lean torrent
and the mad crickets go crazy.

It is the wind that filled my empty hands, the sky.
The night is a lemon tree: yellow, sweet lights.

Tonight she came back to play hide and seek with me.
And with eyes, the poem with tears dives
above the crags, above a procession of hills.

In the village, a tiny casket — moving.
There are priests; white flowers, to the west,
to the east; the way I toss, the way I can't go to sleep.

When my sister comes back from the dead she hides
in my head, and we tumble. Among the corn husks
running, bare feet.

Tonight there was a war in my bed, the way it happened
before.
The way it is happening now, the earth moves and I
look down into a well in which the sun has drowned.

Fuoco

for Franceline

There is a room in the heart of our planet.
The word 'light' lives in it.

Friendship is my dialect's alphabet.
Love is our poetry, our heartbeat. And we love it,
the way we love to say: 'We love ourselves!'

The sun has arrived
and the yellow and light-blue boats.
And the poem that follows the seasons leaps
in my lap, the way sunlight comes out of the closet,
like a squirrel, at dawn.

This is the planet I hurl, down the hill,
over a velvet carpet, around the legs of young trees,
through fresh bodies of water, but if you look,
inside my heart there is a riot of fire.

— In the rain,
a long black dress stepped
on the wharf, crowned with tousled hair
of willow trees,   in the wind —

She left. And with her went what can never come back,
a lifetime. Deprived of future, the planet becomes
cold memory, when hope dies. It burned me.
Inside.

But there are seasons, when the stairs of the crimson
trees break loose, when I fall
to arrive at myself.

To recover our planet, I open my arms
and, like the wake of a ship, my alphabet gushes out
to kiss the flames, my heart, to restore my heartbeat,
the light that smiles in the room
all rooms rush into,   to make more room.

Si sì veru poeta

Si sì veru poeta di Marsigghia
Ndivinimi stu dubbiu e ndi scumbogghia:

Dimmi cu senza peri fa camminu
Dimmi cu ti saluta di luntanu
Dimmi cu mbivi acqua e piscia vinu
Dimmi cu si currumpi e sempr'è sanu.

La viti mbivi acqua e piscia vinu
La littira ti saluta di luntanu
La navi senza peri fa camminu
Lu mari si currumpi e sempr'è sanu.

If You're A True Poet

If you're a true poet of Marseilles
Solve these riddles so there's no doubt.

Tell me who does its journeying with no feet
Tell me who sends you greetings from afar
Tell me who drinks water and urinates wine
Tell me who while breaking remains intact.

The grapevine drinks water and urinates wine
The letter sends you greetings from afar
The ship does its journeying with no feet
The sea as it breaks remains intact.

Amicizia

And I've seen
everything

help; though sometimes this music plays
hide and seek, and our planet
always delights to feel

our bare
feet, and loneliness, that place
in the heart running out
of breath, everything helps;

but only friendship cares, now
that I'm young and stripped at last down
to the man, I know

that a bridge is a somersault
across the ice, that a ladder is a flight
of flesh in the air that I breathe

that you love to save my life, the way
only friendship cares, that you climb, with me,
to the edge of the earth, like one butterfly. Clinging
to a cliff

Doors

Places we go through
to come from

Release the Sun

To the children

Poetry is about learning about sailing a boat
  in the rain
  in the rain and one acre of light
blue water changed to silver: the scales of the river
the colour of mirrors in turmoil.
                        There were women!
and flowers and mirrors and our women are nothing;
and I am in love in the rain. And my thoughts
go back home each time I'm alone.

In the rain we run indoors to the fire:
to the women who followed our men all over the world,
to the strawberries my mother was sharing with us.
                   There were men!
and dreams and colours and our men are nothing;
and I am a poet holding a mirror, in the rain, at night,
and there is our comet: harbour of light.

The way I remember it, there were holes in our sandals,
but a glass planet under our raw flesh, burning,
like the heart of the son of a man
          inside the body of a woman.

There were children!
and life and prayers we share and our children are
nothing; and I am alone in a boat, with the hard music
of tear drops, and our planet: a shattering body of silver.

And there is the world the way we want it:
   the word
   'dawn' echoes through our hearts, a surprise
of fire arrives, rising with the colours of flowers, slowly
flooding the air like an angelic cosmic prayer.

Life is about learning about flying a planet
   at night
   at night and I am a man learning about my heart
about this turbulent light. And it's night. And a mirror
flies home, in the rain, to release the sun.

Country, Culture and Context: Re-inventing the Canadian Poetic Voice

'Country, Culture and Context: Re-inventing The Canadian Poetic Voice' is a compilation of radio interviews given by the poet and aired on CKLN-FM (hosted by Joey Taylor, University of Ottawa, September 22, 1988), on CRUO-FM (hosted by Ruth Bastedo, October 3, 1988), and on CHRW-FM (University of Western Ontario, from *Dreamscapes*, produced by Tim McLaughlin, hosted by Otte Rosenkrantz, December 12, 1988). It was first printed in *Acta Victoriana*, Vol. 113, Number 2, April 1989.

I

A very unusual design for an LP

The cover of *The Way I Remember It* is a very natural representation of a historical moment experienced by many people. The photograph is of my mother, myself and my brother in a village in rural Calabria. At the time, I was five or six years old, shortly after my sister had died. And, of course, there is no father. The father is gone.

On the cover, you have the mother and the children in the rural setting against the wall of a house in the village. Along the border of one of the sides of the LP is this terrifying structure: a building of a metropolis, of a city. We used it because we thought it was very representative of what has actually happened to many people who have come to those crossroads — that threshold when a rural population unknowingly has to leave everything they knew upon entering a new space — the city. This happened to many people living just north of Toronto, for example, and to the people of Newfoundland, or to generally anyone who has left a rural habitat and moved to the city. The city is, of course, a place where people can now expertly manage to look after themselves extremely well. So, we run to the city and not just for economic reasons but for other reasons also.

But going to the city means that we have to deal with the fact that we are very new there. The city doesn't often give us sufficient time to re-orient ourselves, to cope with the new topology, with the new geography, with the new ways of being. Therefore, the last to arrive is usually the most marginalized, the most coerced, the least prepared, and the most exploitable. The photograph represents us on the threshold of the metropolis — in the next five seconds these three people, and the woman who is also pregnant with a third child, will be stepping, irreversibly, into this other order of things, for which they have absolutely no preparation.

* * *

Calabria is a place at the southernmost part of the peninsula that we know of as Italy, that in the nineteenth century, after the unification of Italy, experienced an apocalypse of sorts that still persists today as a result of the people being forced to leave the impoverishment. In Canada, there are probably more Calabrians than in Calabria. There are probably one hundred to one hundred and fifty thousand people in Canada whose background, whose place of origin, is in Calabria. This happened as part of the post-industrial flood to the city and the death of the rural world.

Calabria was a place that a lot of people called home, since the days when it had been a colony of Greece. It was the Magna Graecia. Homer speaks of Charybdis and the voyage of Ulysses through the seas of Calabria. This is the residue of the memory, of the cultural imagination, of Calabrians, as to who they are, even abroad.

* * *

Writing began as an awareness of a catastrophe. I came to Canada in 1961, eleven years old, and spent most of the early years working in different places: car washing in the ice and snow and the ditches of that time — you know, the car washes were not automated then. On Saturday we would go out to the car wash and be dipped into a ditch, and we would be knocking ice off the cars. I say this as a referent because some years later, when I graduated from the university, I got a job working in Paris. I realized very quickly that I couldn't do very much in a job — the impulse to work towards a career wasn't there for me. I needed to go and visit the place I had come from, to determine who I was, and what had happened. When I arrived in the village, well, all the people that I thought would still be there, were gone.

All the inhabitants of my memory had gone everywhere, all over Europe. I got some addresses from my grandmother — who was among the few relatives left in the village — and went off to Northern Italy where some of my relatives were. I then went on to Switzerland, Belgium and France, visiting blood ties, visiting people I had kept in my memory. When I rediscovered them, the picture I had in my imagination of these giant men and wonderful, happy women died. They were now either working in a mine shaft and dying of cancer, or underground, parking cars. One of these trips lasted about a month and a half.

I didn't go back to work in Paris. I started to write poems along the margins of a novel by Rilke, which I'd bought in the train station in Turin. That's how I started to write.

* * *

My father is a very ancient man. Actually, I remember that my great-grandfather was a hundred and twelve years old when he died. My father, who is now eighty, married very late. He is a man who I did not know very much about. He was fifty years old when he had migrated to Canada in 1958; I was simply too young to know what and who he was. By the time I met him I simply did not have a vision of him; for example, I couldn't imagine him as a young man. Therefore, the man I met, and eventually took back as my father again, was a partial self.

When I began my research I discovered that he had had a marvellous past. He could, as could his grandfather, sing and recite ancient poems. In fact, I collected many poems in the Calabrian dialect from him and other Calabrian-Canadians. I also discovered, as did my brother Aldo later on, that in his youth my father had played the Calabrian tambourine, an instrument played with a very particular technique. So, we decided to use the poem 'Si Sì veru poeta di Marsigghia' on the LP.

The poem is a test to the poet in the form of a riddle. In the recording, my father sings the first part in Calabrian and then I sing the second part. The poem, in fact, recalls the Provençal tradition of poetry from which all Western poetry derives. The choice of the Calabrian dialect is very interesting because for years this cultural tradition has had no public voice. That is, all the material that was part of this culture has had no public space. One day, quite accidentally, Aldo discovered that my father could play the tambourine very, very well. Aldo had been spending time looking for someone who could teach him to play the tambourine, and he had contacted someone in New York. Aldo arrived at dinner time one day and he opened the trunk of his car, and there was a tambourine. My father picked it up and started to play.

* * *

'Giovannina' is a poem dedicated to my sister. In fact, it is very close to the reasons for our emigration. The south of Italy, being a very impoverished place, had very few services. One day, when we were children, my sister and I were playing, and she fell on the dirt road and scratched her knee. It became infected, and she died very quickly because they could not find medication. That event, as I remember it, disoriented my father.

Before the disaster, on the terrace of the house there were feasts all the time. But after that, life was without joy. My father realized that this was not a place where he could continue to raise his family. It was then that he decided to start looking for a place to move to, to transfer the family. I remember chasing my father and pulling him by the jacket as he came back from work and having to tell him that he had gone past the house. He couldn't remember where the house was, he kept on going, and I would run after him. He knew that even after the incredible hardships in his life, his suffering during the war, nothing would change. The south of Italy was going to be kept as a marginal area of Italy. This saddened him very much. I think in some way my sister's death was the turning point of our collective experience as a family.

* * *

Borges has influenced me in some way, not so much in his style, not so much in his orientation, but in his thoughts, which have been precise moments of clarity for me. In one place he remarks that 'only new countries have a past, that is to say, an anthropological memory of their past, a living history.' He is comparing, of course, the new country, the Americas, Argentina, in his case, with old Europe. We think of Europe as having history, we think of Europe as the place where history is abundant, inexhaustible, and we think of the Americas, of Canada, as a place that has relatively little history. Of course, this is absolutely absurd. The indigenous people have been on this continent for over twenty thousand years.

The people who then appropriated the continent, the Europeans, have been here for a relatively short time... but they too have their past, it too as old as time. Now what does this mean? This means that we can continue in the modernist project to imagine that man begins his life anew from nothing, here in America, or that he is in fact a land animal who has always inhabited all of the planet. Having said that man is a land animal, we know that culture is a result of living in one place or another on the planet. This is why, for example, we have myths of the sea by people who had a habitat by the sea or myths of the mountain, if the mountain is where they made their home.

Anthropology is in constant transformation and man is in a constant voyage around the planet. It is often tragic that we cannot share the moments of this incredible anthropological transformation as inhabitants of the North American landscape.

* * *

The record is an outgrowth of a collaboration that was and continues to be intense. My brother, who is a musician, and I have been collaborating for about three years. The choice to make a record was not in any way premeditated. It was only after we had gathered so much material that we began to think about putting some of this together in a package to circulate it.

There are intrinsic reasons why we chose or even thought about packaging music and poetry on an LP. One of the things that can be experienced through the record is the essentially *aural* — created for the ear — character of poetry. This is in contrast to poetry in the modern sense, as a written text for private reading. In archaic Greece, the word *mousiké* designated the art of poetry in its totality, as a union of words and music. Its medium of communication was oral performance to the accompaniment of musical instruments. We are the first generation in the city. We come from a rural context and the rural culture has an oral tradition. We probably express ourselves best or, at least, more fully, more naturally, when we do it orally. It is marvellous that for the first time we succeeded in presenting poetry in a way that reflects our culture more closely — a book could have done justice to the poems themselves, but the presentation is such an intrinsic part of the poetic expression. Not only can the poetry be experienced as written texts — the poems are reprinted with the album — but there is, here, the opportunity to experience the voice.

* * *

My brother Aldo composed and performed most of the music. He also produced the album. There were many musicians of Montreal who helped... for example, Aldo Nova, who was so enthusiastic about the project, he helped a lot. But the people who helped us the most, of course, were my mother and father, who came into the studio for the first time in their lives and took over as if they lived there. Then there was the captivating piano performance to 'Amicizia' by Yves Lapierre: we recorded that poem and the music in one take. I can't say that the major problems were production problems because somehow we could communicate so deeply with Aldo — there weren't any disagreements, there was a more instinctive consensus.

* * *

I must say that the notoriety that the LP is getting was totally unforeseen. We knew something very wonderful had happened because people were responding very closely and were making it theirs, were taking it home and were telling us things about what they were experiencing — their own re-creation of the past, or their own dealing with where they are, what hope is, where tomorrow is, and how yesterday inhabits us. In our case, what inhabited us and what inhabits most people in the metropolis is a rural habitat, a home which was in another place. At the same time, when we remember we re-invent our past, we invent what we need, thereby projecting ourselves into the future. The imagination orients us into the new habitat; these are the mechanisms of the subconscious. When we are at a loss as to who and what we are, we need to tell stories in order to give us hope again, even if they are stories of the past. Stories are of what happened: a way of projecting those ways of being and making them come true in the future.

II

To re-invent the modern world and transform it

We are living in a project. For example, strategists who are planning our future and who define where we should live have told us that only ten percent of Canada is inhabitable. The rest is barren land. Well, the fact is that people have been living in the far reaches of Northern Canada for a long time. So, you see how incredibly hideous such thinking is…. I mean, it must be so offensive to the indigenous people, the people who were here before us all, to say that their habitat is uninhabitable. What is the long-term effect of a perspective that views the original peoples and their habitat as nonessential? The same goes for any number of other projections that are similarly based on stereotypical thinking, with regard to the question of our national identity. How do we invent the future? Or, how do I see a re-invention of the future? We have to, once again, question the strategists' modernist project, question the mythologizing of the exclusivistic type of city we would live in. We must find imaginative ways to *reintegrate*, into the mythology of our metropolis, our country, all the people that are living in it.

III

The destruction of a house

Well, no, not the destruction, rather the collapse of the house. The end of the world. That is to say, looking back, people may have a sense that they were inhabiting a place that they could call home, and that their emigration to the city was in fact a catastrophe, as far as the anthropological house is concerned, as far as *home* is concerned. Neither is it a question of how quickly one can assimilate the new habitat, or how quickly one can re-construct even an economic well-being in the new place.

The body has to regain those feelings of belonging. This cannot be achieved through the mind. The body is an anthropology, a geography of emotions. Political feelings towards a new place may develop very quickly; this is a cultural attribute, however, not to be confused with the passion that goes with the sensation of belonging to a place. To make little of the emotional, psychological and anthropological fears of being swallowed up, devoured by the city, that in our time has exploded into a mega-metropolis, is to really not want to understand something very deep about ourselves as living creatures.

* * *

We have employed many strategies to survive the dislocation. These strategies have increasingly tended towards simplification. In this last century, we have adopted the idea that the separate individual is the most important thread of the human fabric. The idea that the individual has to assert himself/herself against all others to survive is a product of the rise of capitalism. It is a paradoxical invention whose impact on the integral survival of life on the planet now becomes of grave concern to us all.

If the question were not merely to survive but to live, then we should abandon survivalist models and begin to re-invent life from the point of view of interdependence. The focusing on the man, on the woman, on the children as separate entities, can be very defeating. Yes, you can assert yourself as an individual, but where is that matrix of emotion that makes life worth living for the whole? *The Way I Remember It* stresses collectivity, or collective values, and it becomes evident to me that the emotional field and the needs of living men, women and children are part and parcel of the same integral genealogical whole.

Notes

Liner Notes on the Album

Produced by Aldo Mazza.
Recording studios: Studio Tempo, Studio Multisons.
Recording engineers: François DesChamps, Daniel Vermette, Frédérique Salter.
Mixing Studio: Studio Aldo Nova.
Mixed by Aldo Mazza.
Mixing engineer: Steven Segal.
'Amicizia': Piano performance by Yves Lapierre.
'Si sì veru poeta di Marsigghia': Tambourine performance by Domenico Mazza. Vocals by Angela Busceti and Domenico Mazza.
Executive producer Antonino Mazza.
All texts © 1988, Antonino Mazza.
All rights reserved through CAPAC.
All music © 1988, Aldo Mazza.
All rights reserved through CAPAC (except for 'Fuoco', Music by Pat Metheny & Lyle Mays © BMI and 'Release the Sun', Music by John Mills-Cockel © Procan).

We gratefully acknowledge the assistance of the Secretary of State for Multiculturalism, Government of Canada, and Primo di Luca & Associates, Downsview, Canada.
Special thanks to Eli Mandel, Adele Wiseman, Aldo Nova, Yves Lapierre, Barbara Preston, Réper-

cussion, Artscorp, Alfredo Romano, Mario Romano, Haygo Demir, Hratch Arabian, Claudia Katri, Patrick Crean, Lorraine Monk, Margaret Anne Kearns, Antonio D'Alfonso, Tonya Lockyer, Patrick White, Jean-Antonin Billard, Gerald Owen, Yvonne Brandy, Giovanna & Mario, and Vittorio for their confidence and support.

Manufactured and Distributed by P © Trans-Verse Productions, P.O. Box 333, Station A, Montreal, Quebec, H3C 2S1 Canada; P.O. Box 892, Station P, Toronto, Ontario, M5S 2Z2 Canada. To order *The Way I Remember It* write Trans-Verse Productions.)

Designed by Linzi Bartolini, Bruce Mau Design Inc.

Acknowledgements

Acknowledgements are made to the following magazines and anthologies where some of these poems have appeared: *Poesis, Poetry Australia* (Australia), *Anthos, Italian Americana* (USA), *Canadian Literature, Spazio Umano* (Italy), *The Poetic Village* (1975, USA), *Roman Candles* (1978), *Italian Canadian Voices* (1984), and *Canadian Travellers in Italy* (Exile Editions, 1989).

The Way I Remember It (ISBN 0-021710-00-3) was first published in 1988 by Trans-Verse Productions, P. O. Box 892, Station P, Toronto, ON., M5S 2Z2.

'Country, Culture and Context: Re-inventing the Canadian Poetic Voice' was originally printed in *Acta Victoriana* (1989), ed. Emma Thom and Elias Polizoes.

We would also like to thank John Strati, *The Montreal Mirror*; Elettra Bedon, *Il Cittadino Canadese* (Montreal); Bart Grooms, *Option Magazine* (Los Angeles, CA); Clément Trudel, *Le Devoir* (Montreal); William Anselmi, *Vice Versa*; Tim McLaughlin, *Air Shift* (London); Andrée Laurier, *The Canadian Composer/Le Compositeur canadien*; Burt Heward, *The Ottawa Citizen*; David Giguère, *Articles* (Ottawa); Anna Foschi, *L'Eco d'Italia* (Vancouver); Mary Di Michele, *The Toronto Star, Saturday Magazine; Il Corriere*

Canadese (Toronto); *L'Ora di Ottawa*; François Bergeron, *L'Express de Toronto*; and Luisa Del Giudice (UCLA), for reviews of *The Way I Remember It*.

We are especially grateful to Peter Gzowski, *Morningside*, CBC; Ken Rockburn, CHEZ-FM (Ottawa); Brent Bambury, *Brave New Waves*, CBC; CFMB (Montreal); John Kalina, *Daybreak*, CBC; Michael Gravel, CKCU-FM (Carleton University); Josie Panetta, CHIN (Toronto); CHRW-FM (University of Western Ontario); Ruth Bastedo, CFUO-FM (University of Ottawa); CKDU-FM (Dalhousie University, Halifax); Joey Taylor, CKLN-FM, Ryerson Radio (Toronto); Russel Powell, CIUT-FM (University of Toronto); Stan Solway, CBC (Toronto); Martin Deck, CJAM-FM (University of Windsor); Q101-FM (Smiths Falls); MTV (Toronto); CFRU-FM (University of Guelph); CKUT-FM (McGill University) and Co-op Radio (Vancouver) for airing interviews with the author. And to CKLN-FM (Toronto), CHRW-FM (London), WFMU-FM (Uppsala College, East Orange, NJ), KGNU-FM (Boulder, CO), KCRW-FM (Santa Monica, CA), WCSB-FM (Cleveland), WCBN-FM (Ann Arbor, MI) where *The Way I Remember It* was ranked among their most aired recordings for 1988 and 1989.

The Vancouver-based Dance Company, EDAM, has used parts of *The Way I Remember It* in a dance choreography by Peter Bingham, entitled *Inside Out*.

By the Same Author

Structures of Chaos
(1979)

The Bones of Cuttlefish
(Translation of *Ossi di seppia*
by Eugenio Montale, 1983)

The First Paradise, Odetta...
(Translated, and with a Homage
to Pier Paolo Pasolini, 1985)

The Way I Remember It
(Poetry album with musician Aldo Mazza, 1988)

Pier Paolo Pasolini: Poetry
(Selected and translated, with an afterword, 1991)

About the Author

Antonino Mazza, poet, translator and editor, was born in Calabria, Italy, and came to Canada in 1961. He studied at Carleton University, La Scuola Normale Superiore in Pisa, and the University of Toronto. He has taught at the University of Ottawa, and at Queen's University, Kingston, Ontario. As editor he has been associated with *Anthos* (a magazine he co-founded in 1978), *Vice Versa* and *Gamut International*. His poems, essays and literary translations have appeared in numerous magazines, journals and anthologies in Canada, the United States, Australia and Italy. His spokensongs have been choreographed for dance, widely performed and discussed in the context of North American ethnic literature and postmodernism. He lives in Toronto.

Printed by
Ateliers Graphiques Marc Veilleux Inc.
Cap-Saint-Ignace Qué.
in November 1992